THE LITTLE BOOK OF

SINGAPORE

FOOD *Illustrated*

Our Favourite Treats From A to Z

EMILY YEO
Illustrated by
Benjamin Wang

Marshall Cavendish
Editions

Published by Marshall Cavendish Editions
An imprint of Marshall Cavendish International

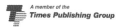
A member of the
Times Publishing Group

Other Marshall Cavendish Offices:
Marshall Cavendish Corporation, 800 Westchester Ave, Suite N-641,
Rye Brook, NY 10573, USA • Marshall Cavendish International (Thailand)
Co Ltd, 253 Asoke, 16th Floor, Sukhumvit 21 Road, Klongtoey Nua,
Wattana, Bangkok 10110, Thailand • Marshall Cavendish (Malaysia)
Sdn Bhd, Times Subang, Lot 46, Subang Hi-Tech Industrial Park,
Batu Tiga, 40000 Shah Alam, Selangor Darul Ehsan, Malaysia

Marshall Cavendish is a registered trademark of Times Publishing Limited

National Library Board, Singapore Cataloguing in Publication Data
Name(s): Yeo, Emily. | Wang, Benjamin, illustrator.
Title: The little book of Singapore food illustrated : our favourite treats
from A to Z / Emily Yeo ; illustrated by Benjamin Wang.
Other Title(s): Singapore food illustrated
Description: Singapore : Marshall Cavendish Editions, [2022]
Identifier(s): ISBN 978-981-4868-72-3
Subject(s): LCSH: Cooking, Singaporean.
Classification: DDC 641.595957--dc23

Printed in Singapore

CONTENTS

INTRODUCTION

As one of the worst cooks I know, writing a cookbook is the last thing on my bucket list. And thankfully, a cookbook, this is not! Instead, this is my little labour of love, highlighting and underscoring the myriad lessons I've gleaned from my years running the culinary studio, The Little Things.

Having worked with numerous young chefs, mostly less than three feet tall, I've cultivated a knack for breaking down complex recipes into more digestible bite-size morsels for the benefit of these little ones.

I've also amassed a collection of favourite local recipes from talking food all day long with people from all walks of life. And of course, through it all, I've also sharpened my skills in the kitchen.

Teaming up with Ben, my amazing illustrator, was a natural process as he brought all these local delights to life. For truly, each of these dishes, listed from A to Z, have so much more to convey than just a mere recipe. There is a story, a fun fact, a learning point and a whole process of putting the dish together!

I hope that people of all ages, backgrounds and cultures will enjoy this little book, from uncovering more about popular snacks and discovering new treats, to enjoying the engaging illustrations and appreciating the treasure trove of lessons that can be found in the kitchen. I believe there is a little something for everyone in this *Little Book of Singapore Food Illustrated.*

Bon appétit!

ANG KU KUEH

Ang ku kueh literally means red tortoise cake in Hokkien. It is a very symbolic dish because red represents good luck, while tortoises are representative of long life. As such, *ang ku kueh*, shaped like a tortoise shell, is often presented as an auspicious food gift to celebrate a baby's first month or the birthday of an elderly person. Let's try making our own!

SOFT CHEWY SKIN MADE FROM GLUTINOUS RICE FLOUR

SWEET FILLING MADE FROM MUNG BEANS OR PEANUTS

NATURAL LINER USING FRAGRANT BANANA LEAF

INGREDIENTS

Makes about 8 pieces

150 g glutinous rice flour + extra for dusting mould

2 Tbsp sugar

⅛ tsp salt

15 g red dragon fruit blended with 55 ml water

125 ml water

3 Tbsp cooking oil + more for brushing on banana leaves

Banana leaves, cut into small rectangles the size of the *kueh*

200 g store-bought mung bean paste

PREPARE THE DOUGH

1. Combine the glutinous rice flour, sugar and salt in a mixing bowl.

2. Place the dragon fruit juice and water in a pan. Bring to a boil.

3. Pour the hot liquid over the flour mixture in the mixing bowl.

4. Stir with a spoon until a soft, shiny dough is achieved.

5. Cover dough with cling wrap and let it rest for 10 minutes.

SHAPE THE KUEH

1. Divide the filling into 8 parts and roll into balls. Repeat with the dough.

2. Flatten a ball of dough. Place a ball of filling in the centre and enclose.

3. Dust the *ang ku kueh* mould well with flour to prevent sticking.

4. Gently press the dough ball into the mould.

5. Tap and knock the mould to remove the *kueh*.

6. Place the *kueh* on an oiled banana leaf. Repeat with the remaining ingredients.

NOTE: The amount of dough and filling to use will depend on the size of the mould.

STEAM THE KUEH

1. Place the *kueh* in a steamer. Bring the water to a boil over high heat. When the water is boiling, lower the heat to medium.

2. Steam the *kueh* for 12–15 minutes until the colour of the *kueh* changes and the dough is cooked.

3. Brush the cooked *kueh* with cooking oil, then set aside to cool completely before enjoying.

KITCHEN FUN FACTS

STEAMING

At 100°C, water turns into steam. Steam can be used to cook many types of food from cakes to seafood!

Ang ku kueh is traditionally steamed in bamboo steamers, but steaming can also be done using a pot or wok with a lid and a steaming rack.

Always be extra careful though as steam can scald.

BUBBLE TEA

Undoubtedly Singapore's unofficial favourite dessert beverage! The bubble tea craze hit Singapore in the early 2000s and bubble tea outlets literally popped up in every corner of Singapore! Twenty years on, the beverage remains one of Singapore's favourite drinks! What makes bubble tea extra special is the irresistible chewy little balls called pearls. These balls are made from tapioca flour and aren't all that difficult to make at home! Shall we try?

INGREDIENTS

Makes 3-4 servings

4 Tbsp water

2 Tbsp brown sugar

85 g tapioca flour + more for dusting

SPECIAL WIDE STRAW FOR SUCKING UP PEARLS; USE REUSABLE STRAWS IF YOU CAN!

TYPICALLY ENJOYED WITH FRAGRANT AND CREAMY ICED MILK TEA

YUMMY CHEWY TRANSLUCENT BALLS SWEETENED WITH BROWN SUGAR

PREPARE THE PEARLS

1. Heat the water in a pan over medium heat. Add the brown sugar and stir until dissolved.

2. Turn off the heat and add half the tapioca flour. Stir until the mixture is smooth.

3. Turn on the heat again and stir the mixture until it is thickened.

4. Remove the pan from heat. Add the remaining tapioca flour and mix to get a sticky dough.

5. Dust a work surface with tapioca flour and knead the dough until it is soft and elastic.

6. Roll the dough out into thin logs about the same thickness as a bubble tea straw.

7. Using a dough cutter, cut the rolls into small pieces.

8. Roll the pieces between your palms into balls.

9. Boil a pot of water and add the pearls. Boil until the pearls float. Remove with a slotted spoon and add to your favourite beverage!

TRY THESE COMBINATIONS!

TAPIOCA PEARLS IN CHOCOLATE MILK

TAPIOCA PEARLS IN BANDUNG

TAPIOCA PEARLS IN BLUE PEA LEMONADE

KITCHEN FUN FACTS

TAPIOCA FLOUR

As we work in the kitchen, we'll come across many types of flours. In the recipe for tapioca pearls, the flour required is tapioca flour. How is tapioca flour produced?

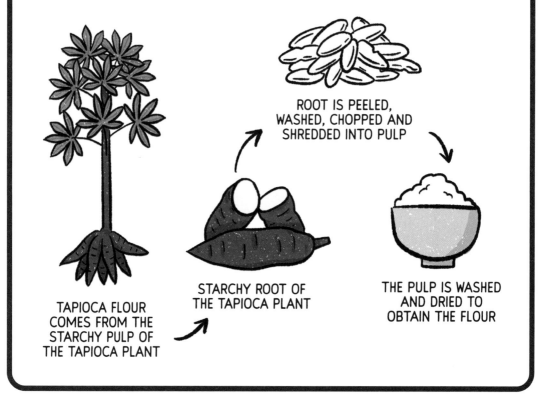

ROOT IS PEELED, WASHED, CHOPPED AND SHREDDED INTO PULP

STARCHY ROOT OF THE TAPIOCA PLANT

THE PULP IS WASHED AND DRIED TO OBTAIN THE FLOUR

TAPIOCA FLOUR COMES FROM THE STARCHY PULP OF THE TAPIOCA PLANT

CURRY PUFFS

Many cultures have similar pastries, from the British Cornish pasty and Portuguese empanada, to the Indian samosa and Malay *epok epok*. This snack can be either deep-fried or baked. In Singapore, many favour curry puffs with a crispy, buttery shortcrust pastry. Here is a recipe for a delicious curry puff that can be quickly whipped up using frozen puff pastry.

CRISPY FLAKY BUTTERY SKIN

TRADEMARK CRIMPED EDGE

SPICY POTATO CURRY

A WEDGE OF HARDBOILED EGG

SOMETIMES WITH SARDINES

INGREDIENTS

Makes 4 curry puffs

4 Tbsp cooking oil

2 cloves garlic, peeled and finely chopped

1 onion, peeled and chopped

3 sprigs curry leaves, plucked, stems discarded

3 Tbsp curry powder, mixed with a little water into a paste

1 tsp sugar

150 ml water

100 ml chicken stock

Salt to taste

300 g potatoes, peeled and cut into small cubes

4 sheets frozen prata

1 hardboiled egg, peeled and cut into 4 wedges

1 egg, beaten for egg wash

PREPARE THE FILLING

1. Heat the oil in a pan over medium heat. Add the garlic, onion and curry leaves. Sauté until the onion is softened.

2. Add the curry paste and mix well. Sauté until fragrant.

3. Add the water, chicken stock and salt. Simmer over low heat.

4. Add the potatoes and simmer until tender. Let cool before using.

FORM THE CURRY PUFF

1. Preheat the oven to 200°C. Remove the frozen prata from the freezer one sheet a time, just before using.

2. Spoon a quarter of the filling onto the prata. Add a wedge of hardboiled egg. Fold the prata to enclose the filling. Crimp the edges to seal. Repeat to make another 3 puffs.

BAKE THE CURRY PUFFS

1. Brush the curry puffs with egg wash. Place on a baking tray.

2. Bake the curry puffs for 10–15 minutes until golden brown.

KITCHEN FUN FACTS

AROMATICS

Ah, the mouthwatering scents! Can you smell them already? Cooks utilise aromatics, consisting of herbs, spices and vegetables, to add flavour to dishes. In curry puffs, these aromatics are garlic, onion and curry leaves!

Below are examples of other aromatics typically used in stocks and stews.

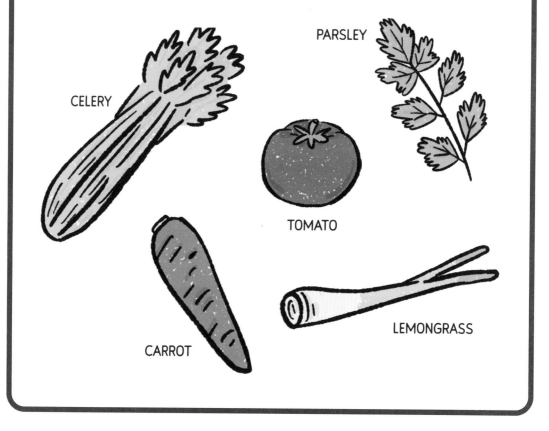

CELERY

PARSLEY

TOMATO

CARROT

LEMONGRASS

DURIAN CAKE

What's a fruit that's nasty to touch yet sweet to eat? The durian! It is often dubbed as "the smelliest fruit in the world", but at the same time, it is also known as "the king of fruits". Durian season is between June and September, and you'll see many stalls selling durians in Singapore during that time. You'll probably even be able to smell the durians as you drive down the road with your windows down. Besides eating the fruit, you can also enjoy durian baked in a cake.

SOFT AND CREAMY
YELLOW FLESH

A LAYER
OF CREAMY
DURIAN PUREE
TOPPING

TRADEMARK
SPIKY HUSK

FLUFFY AND
FRAGRANT
BUTTER CAKE

INGREDIENTS

Makes one 20-cm square cake

175 g unsalted butter,
   at room temperature

150 g caster sugar

2 large eggs

150 g durian flesh,
   at room temperature,
   blended until smooth

1 tsp vanilla essence

$1/8$ tsp salt

150 g plain flour

1 tsp baking powder

4 Tbsp full cream milk,
   at room temperature

PREPARE THE BATTER

1. Preheat the oven to 160°C. Line a 20-cm square baking tray. Set aside.

2. Place the butter in a mixing bowl and beat lightly for 2-3 minutes to fluff it up.

3. Add the sugar and beat with an electric mixer until the mixture is light and fluffy.

4. Add the eggs one at a time. Mix well after each addition. It is important to mix well at this stage.

5. Add the durian, vanilla essence and salt and mix well.

6. Add the milk and mix well.

7. Combine the flour and baking powder in another bowl. Mix well.

8. Sift the flour mixture into the batter. Fold in gently, until combined.

9. Pour the batter into the lined baking tray. Tap the bottom of the tray to release any air bubbles.

BAKE THE CAKE

1. Bake for 45 minutes or until a skewer inserted into the centre of the cake comes out clean.

2. Remove from the oven and set aside to cool for an hour before serving.

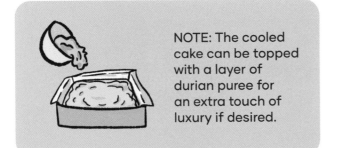

NOTE: The cooled cake can be topped with a layer of durian puree for an extra touch of luxury if desired.

KITCHEN FUN FACTS

WHISKING

A whisk is used to introduce air to ingredients. Whisking well when baking is important so the resulting baked goods are airy, light and fluffy. Whisking also helps blend and combine ingredients together smoothly.

There are several types of whisks available: the hand whisk, the handheld electric whisk and the stand mixer. Choose the right one for your task.

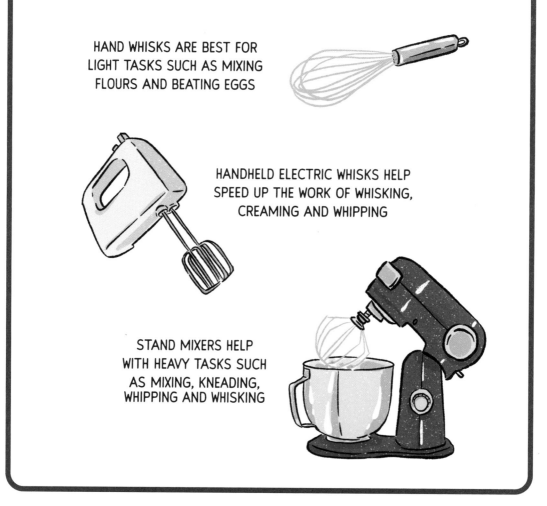

HAND WHISKS ARE BEST FOR LIGHT TASKS SUCH AS MIXING FLOURS AND BEATING EGGS

HANDHELD ELECTRIC WHISKS HELP SPEED UP THE WORK OF WHISKING, CREAMING AND WHIPPING

STAND MIXERS HELP WITH HEAVY TASKS SUCH AS MIXING, KNEADING, WHIPPING AND WHISKING

EGG TARTS

With a crisp, flaky crust and a smooth, silky custard, egg tarts are our favourite any time snack. But where did the egg tart originate from? It has been said that the first egg tart was created in a restaurant in Guangzhou, China. However, the egg tart is also very similar to a popular Portuguese pastry known as *pastel de nata*, which found its way to Macau. Whichever way it might be, we're just glad someone brought that first egg tart to Singapore!

CRISP AND
FLAKY GOLDEN
BROWN CRUST

LIGHTLY SWEETENED,
SMOOTH AND
CREAMY
EGG CUSTARD

INGREDIENTS

Makes 5 egg tarts

CRUST

60 g butter, at
   room temperature

15 g icing sugar

½ egg, beaten

1 drop vanilla essence

100 g plain flour

5 g cake flour

EGG CUSTARD

150 ml hot water

50 g caster sugar

2 eggs

75 ml evaporated milk

1 drop vanilla essence

PREPARE THE CRUST

1. Beat the butter and icing sugar until smooth and creamy. Add the egg, a little at a time. Mix in the vanilla.

2. Sift the flours into another bowl, then add to the butter mixture in two batches. Knead into a dough.

3. Roll the dough out on a floured work surface into a 0.5-cm thick sheet. Cut the dough into circles slightly larger than the moulds. Gently press the pastry into the moulds.

MAKE THE CUSTARD

1. Add the sugar to the hot water and stir until the sugar is dissolved.

2. Whisk the eggs with the evaporated milk. Add the sugar syrup and mix gently.

3. Strain the egg mixture to ensure the custard is smooth.

BAKE THE TARTS

1. Preheat the oven to 200°C. Pour the egg mixture evenly into the prepared moulds and place on a baking tray.

2. Bake for 15 minutes, then lower the oven temperature to 180°C and bake for another 15 minutes or until the crust is golden brown.

KITCHEN FUN FACTS

OVEN SAFETY

Always be careful when working with hot stoves and ovens. Even experienced cooks and bakers can end up with burns as it only takes a moment of carelessness to get hurt! Here are some things to remember when using the oven.

PUT ON BAKING GLOVES TO
PROTECT YOUR HANDS AND
FINGERS WHEN USING THE OVEN

USE BOTH HANDS WHEN
TAKING BAKING TRAYS IN
AND OUT OF THE OVEN

OPEN AND SHUT THE OVEN DOOR
GENTLY TO PREVENT ITEMS
SUCH AS LOOSE CLOTHING FROM
BEING CAUGHT IN THE DOORS

ALWAYS BE ALERT
WHEN BAKING WITH CHILDREN

FISH BALLS

What kind of ball is bouncy, savoury and oh-so delicious?
Fish balls, of course! These little balls are the perfect
accompaniment to noodle dishes across Singapore,
but finding a good quality fish ball might not be so easy.
Many are highly processed and include additives and
preservatives. The good news though is that fish balls aren't
all that difficult to make at home! Shall we try?

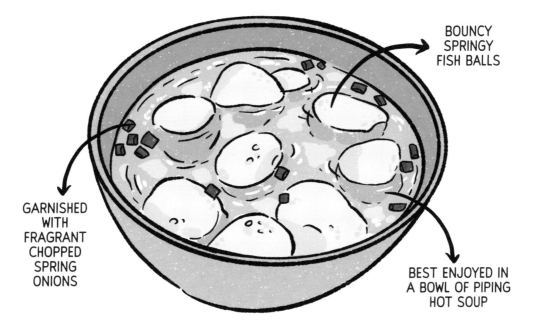

BOUNCY
SPRINGY
FISH BALLS

GARNISHED
WITH
FRAGRANT
CHOPPED
SPRING
ONIONS

BEST ENJOYED IN
A BOWL OF PIPING
HOT SOUP

INGREDIENTS

Makes 25–30 fish balls

500 g white fish meat, from
    Spanish mackerel or yellowfin

1 tsp salt

1 tsp ground white pepper

2 tsp sugar

5 Tbsp tapioca flour

MAKE THE FISH BALLS

1. Mince the fish meat into a paste using the spine of a cleaver.

2. Add the salt and pepper, sugar and tapioca flour and mix well. Scoop the paste up with one hand and throw it back into the bowl. Repeat until the paste is smooth and glossy.

3. Using wet hands, grab a handful of fish paste and squeeze it through your thumb and forefinger. Scoop the paste up with a spoon and place in a large bowl of water. Repeat until the paste is used up. Strain the fish balls and cook in a pot of boiling water. The fish balls will float when done.

KITCHEN FUN FACTS

MINCING

When we mince an ingredient, we are chopping it into fine pieces. For wet ingredients like fish, mincing will give it a pasty texture.

A good tool to use for mincing meat is a cleaver or a heavy knife. Alternatively, the meat can also be minced using a blender or food processor.

GORENG PISANG

Why are bananas never lonely? Because they hang out in bunches! The same is true for *goreng pisang* or banana fritters. You can't just eat one! Made by coating fragrant ripe bananas in a light batter, then deep-frying to golden brown perfection, *goreng pisang* is best eaten freshly fried, but tastes good cooled too.

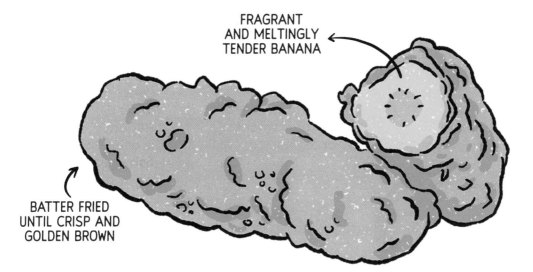

FRAGRANT AND MELTINGLY TENDER BANANA

BATTER FRIED UNTIL CRISP AND GOLDEN BROWN

INGREDIENTS

Makes 2-3 servings

60 g self-raising flour

28 g corn flour

1 Tbsp rice flour

½ tsp baking powder

⅛ tsp salt

90 ml iced water

4–6 firm, ripe bananas (see page 31 for a list of bananas for frying)

Cooking oil for deep-frying

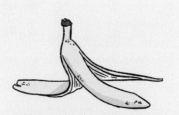

NOTE: Banana peel has many uses, so don't be too quick to throw it away! It can be used as fertiliser and can even be used to polish shoes!

PREPARE THE BATTER

1. Combine the self-raising flour, corn flour, rice flour, baking powder and salt in a mixing bowl.

2. Add the iced water gradually while whisking until the batter is smooth.

3. Peel the bananas and leave whole or slice in half lengthways. Place in the batter and let sit for 5-10 minutes.

FRY THE FRITTERS

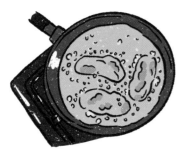

1. Heat the oil. Gently lower 2-3 pieces of banana into the hot oil, being careful not to overcrowd the pot.

2. When the fritters turn golden brown, remove with a wire strainer. Drain well on paper towels. Serve hot.

THE BEST BANANAS FOR FRYING

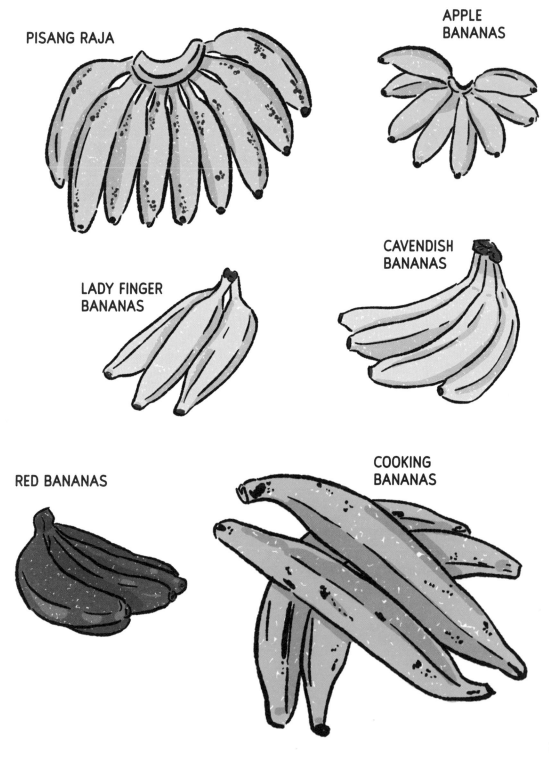

PISANG RAJA

APPLE BANANAS

LADY FINGER BANANAS

CAVENDISH BANANAS

RED BANANAS

COOKING BANANAS

KITCHEN FUN FACTS

DEEP-FRYING

What's the secret to a good *goreng pisang*? Deep-frying! When the bananas are coated in batter and placed into hot oil, a crust quickly forms on the outside. This keeps the bananas moist inside.

To test if the oil is at the right temperature for frying, dip a dry wooden chopstick into the oil. If bubbles start to form steadily around the chopstick, it is at the right temperature. If the bubbles form quickly and vigorously, the oil is too hot. Turn off the heat and let the oil cool before heating again.

Be very careful when deep-frying as oil can splatter when it gets too hot. Always watch the heat and never allow the oil to get overheated.

HAINANESE CHICKEN RICE

When the Hainanese immigrants arrived in Singapore in the 19th century, they brought the food of their hometowns with them. One of these dishes was Wenchang chicken, said to be the original Hainanese chicken. With different cooking techniques introduced by cooks over the years, the dish evolved, resulting in the dish that we call our very own today!

SWEET DARK
SOY SAUCE

TENDER,
JUICY
CHICKEN

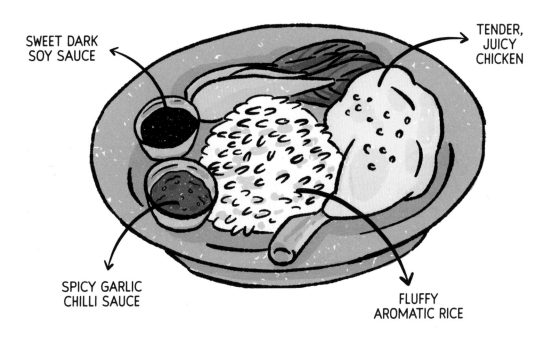

SPICY GARLIC
CHILLI SAUCE

FLUFFY
AROMATIC RICE

INGREDIENTS

Makes 1 serving

CHICKEN

1 chicken thigh

Salt, as needed

1 Tbsp sesame oil

¼ tsp light soy sauce

2-3 slices ginger

1 clove garlic, peeled and sliced

¼ spring onion, chopped

RICE

½ cup long-grain rice

½ Tbsp sesame oil

1 clove garlic, peeled and chopped

1 slice ginger

125 ml chicken stock

4 Tbsp water

GARLIC CHILLI SAUCE

1 red chilli, stem removed

4 garlic cloves, peeled

½ tsp salt

½ tsp sugar

2.5-cm knob ginger, peeled
  and sliced

1 Tbsp light soy sauce

3 Tbsp water

PREPARE THE CHICKEN

 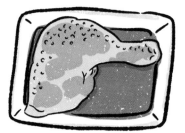 

1. Rub the chicken skin well with salt to remove any impurities. Rinse well with water and pat dry with paper towels.

2. Rub the chicken with sesame oil, light soy sauce and 1 tsp salt. Set aside to marinate.

3. Sprinkle the ginger, garlic and spring onion over the marinated chicken and transfer to a steaming plate. Steam the chicken for 15 minutes or until it is done.

COOK THE RICE

1. Rinse the rice and drain. Add fresh water and leave the rice to soak for 10 minutes.

2. Heat the sesame oil in a wok over medium heat. Add the garlic and ginger and sauté until fragrant.

3. Drain the rice and add to the wok. Stir the rice in the wok for a few minutes to coat the rice grains well with oil.

4. Transfer the rice to a rice cooker. Add the chicken stock and water and cook. Serve the rice with the chicken, side dishes of choice, and garlic chilli sauce and sweet dark soy sauce.

PREPARE THE GARLIC CHILLI SAUCE

1. Place all the ingredients in a blender and blend until smooth.

KITCHEN FUN FACTS

KITCHEN SAFETY AND HYGIENE

Cooking often requires cutting and preparing both raw meats and vegetables, so it is essential that we are aware of the dangers of cross-contamination.

Cross-contamination is the transfer of harmful bacteria from one surface to another. This includes touching raw meat, then handling cooked or ready-to-eat foods without washing your hands, or using the same knife or chopping board to prepare raw and cooked foods.

To prevent cross-contamination, always observe proper hygiene and wash your hands well before preparing food. Use a different set of utensils to prepare different types of foods, and wash thoroughly with soap and hot water.

A good idea would be to label or colour code your chopping boards for different purposes.

ICED GEM BISCUITS

These pretty little biscuits are an all-time favourite among Singaporeans both young and old. Some enjoy the icing and biscuit together in one bite, while others break off the icing and enjoy it separately from the biscuit! Iced gem biscuits are so common here, few know that they were first made by a biscuit manufacturer in the UK way back in the 1900s!

DOLLOP OF HARD ICING IN A RANGE OF PRETTY PASTEL COLOURS

SMALL ROUND BISCUITS THAT ARE SOMETIMES CALLED BELLY BUTTON BISCUITS

INGREDIENTS
Makes about 30 biscuits

BISCUIT
25 g butter

1½ Tbsp caster sugar

1 Tbsp beaten egg

⅛ tsp maple syrup

50 g plain flour

⅛ tsp salt

ICING
290 g icing sugar

2 Tbsp meringue powder

4 Tbsp warm water

Food colouring of choice

MAKE THE BISCUITS

1. Preheat the oven to 180°C. Line a baking tray with baking paper.

2. Place the butter and sugar in a bowl. Beat until light and fluffy.

3. Add the beaten egg and maple syrup. Mix until combined.

4. Sift in the flour and salt and mix until the dough comes together.

5. Dust a work surface with flour and roll the dough out into a 1-cm thick sheet.

6. Use a small round cutter to cut shapes from the dough. Arrange on the baking tray. Bake for 7 minutes or until cookies are done.

PREPARE THE ICING

1. Combine the icing sugar, meringue powder and warm water in a bowl. Beat with an electric whisk until smooth.

2. Add colouring and mix well. Spoon into a piping bag fitted with a piping nozzle. Pipe icing on cookies. Leave to harden before storing or serving.

KITCHEN FUN FACTS

MEASURING TOOLS

When you want to ensure consistency in your cooking and baking, a digital kitchen scale and a set of measuring spoons and cups will come in handy. These tools will help with accuracy when measuring dry and liquid ingredients.

1 TABLESPOON (TBSP)
= 15 ML

1 TEASPOON (TSP)
= 5 ML

1 TABLESPOON (TBSP) = 3 TEASPOONS (TSP)

1 MEASURING CUP = 250 ML

KITCHEN SCALE

COCONUT JAM (KAYA)

Aromatic, sweet and creamy, this is the go-to sandwich spread for many local families at breakfast. The Malay word, *kaya*, means "rich", and is an apt description for this coconut jam flavoured with pandan. This jam is commonly served spread on toast, but is also often enjoyed with soft waffles, prata and other pastries.

KAYA WAFFLE

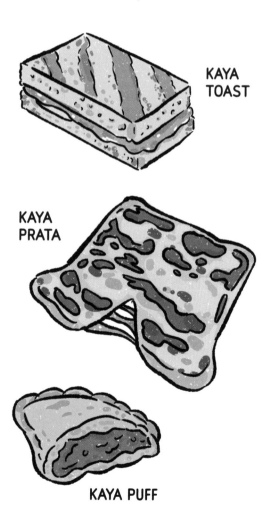

KAYA TOAST

KAYA PRATA

KAYA PUFF

INGREDIENTS

Makes about 200 g

5 pandan leaves, cut into short lengths

5 Tbsp water

220 ml coconut cream

3 Tbsp brown sugar

3 Tbsp white sugar

⅛ tsp salt

5 egg yolks, beaten

MAKE THE KAYA

1. Using a blender, blend the pandan leaves with the water. Strain to get pandan juice.

2. In a pan, mix the pandan juice with the coconut cream, brown sugar, white sugar and salt.

3. Boil pot of water. Sit the pan over the mouth of the pot and stir over low heat until the sugar is dissolved.

4. Remove the pan from heat. Stir in the beaten egg yolks gradually. Mix well.

5. Repeat to stir the mixture over low heat for 30 minutes until it thickens.

6. The *kaya* should have a gooey consistency. Let cool before enjoying.

KITCHEN FUN FACTS

SUGAR

Did you notice that the *kaya* recipe contains a high proportion of sugar? Besides adding sweetness, sugar also acts as a preservative. It helps to bind the moisture from the ingredients, leaving little left in the *kaya* for bacteria growth. When the sugar dissolves and interacts with the other ingredients, it starts to thicken, giving the *kaya* its signature gooey, creamy consistency!

KUEH LAPIS SAGU

Kueh lapis sagu is a traditional steamed cake. It is also known as *gao cang kou* (Cantonese) or *jiu ceng gao* (Chinese), which translates to nine-layer cake. This well-loved snack is enjoyed for its rich and sweet pandan-coconut fragrance and chewy texture. It typically comes in a hue of rainbow colours or in red, green and white. Some savour the *kueh* by peeling the layers off one by one, while others prefer it thinly sliced. The recipe that follows is a simple one for a four-layer cake, but you can double the recipe and have more layers as preferred.

SOFT, TENDER AND CHEWY

CHEERFUL MULTICOLOURED LAYERS

INFUSED WITH THE FLAVOURS OF PANDAN AND COCONUT MILK

INGREDIENTS

Makes 5–6 pieces

100 ml hot water

60 g caster sugar

⅛ tsp salt

100 ml coconut milk

70 g tapioca flour

15 g rice flour

1 drop pandan paste

2 other food colouring of choice

PREPARE THE KUEH

1. Pour 100 ml hot water into a medium bowl. Add the sugar and salt and stir until dissolved. Stir in the coconut milk.

2. Let the mixture cool to room temperature, then stir in the tapioca flour and rice flour. Mix well.

3. Divide the mixture among 4 small bowls. Add pandan paste to 1 bowl and different food colourings to another 2 bowls. Leave the last bowl plain as a white layer.

4. Prepare a steamer. Use a cloth to wrap the lid to prevent condensed water from dripping onto the *kueh*. Lightly oil a 14 x 6-cm steaming tray and place it into the steamer.

5. Stir the mixture well and remove any air bubbles before pouring into the steaming tray.

6. Steam the layer for 5 minutes before adding the next. Repeat this step for each layer. Top the steamer up with boiling water as necessary.

KITCHEN FUN FACTS

MISE EN PLACE

Mise en place (MEEZ ahn plahs) is a French term that refers to setting up your work station before starting to cook or bake. It means to have all your ingredients measured, peeled, cut, chopped, grated or sliced; and your bowls, cooking utensils and equipment at hand, so that they are easily accessible when you need them.

When making *kueh lapis sagu*, your work station would look like this:

100 ML
HOT WATER

60 G SUGAR +
⅛ TSP SALT

100 ML
COCONUT MILK

70 G TAPIOCA FLOUR +
15 G RICE FLOUR

PANDAN PASTE +
FOOD COLOURING

MEASURING CUP

MEDIUM BOWL

4 SMALL BOWLS
AND SPOONS

STEAMER

STEAMING TRAY

LASSI

Have you ever had ice-cold lassi on a hot day?
You've simply got to try it for yourself to know how good it is!
Most Indian restaurants would have their own rendition of a
lassi. It could come in various flavours or in its original flavour.
Lassi is a yoghurt drink flavoured either with blended fruit or
salt. And because its main ingredient is yoghurt, it is full of
health benefits and can help with digestion. That's also why
it is a beverage of choice after heavy and spicy meals.

INGREDIENTS

Makes 1 serving

1 cup fresh mango, cut into
    cubes, chilled

1 cup plain yoghurt, chilled

4 Tbsp milk, chilled

3–4 Tbsp sugar

Seeds from 1 cardamom pod,
    or ¼ tsp ground cardamom
    (optional)

MAKE THE LASSI

THIS HAS GOT TO BE OUR EASIEST RECIPE YET, THANKS TO THE BLENDER!

1. Place the ingredients in a blender and process until smooth.

2. Pour into a glass and enjoy!

KITCHEN FUN FACTS

BLENDERS

Blenders make kitchen work so much easier, from processing, blending, crushing and grinding. Always be careful when handling blenders though as the blades are very sharp

BLENDERS CAN BE USED TO

MIX MILK AND CREAM AT HIGH SPEEDS INTO MILKSHAKES

PROCESS FRUIT AND VEGGIES INTO SMOOTHIES AND PUREES

GRIND NUTS, OATS AND SPICES

CRUSH ICE

MIN JIANG KUEH

Pancakes are a favourite food all over the world. And in Singapore, we have the Chinese *min jiang kueh* (*mian jian gao*) available from hawker stalls all over the island. These thick, yeast-raised pancakes are soft yet firm, tender yet chewy, and come with an assortment of toppings including peanuts and sugar, sweetened grated coconut, and red bean paste. Some stalls also offer new flavours such as green tea, durian, black sesame and even cheese.

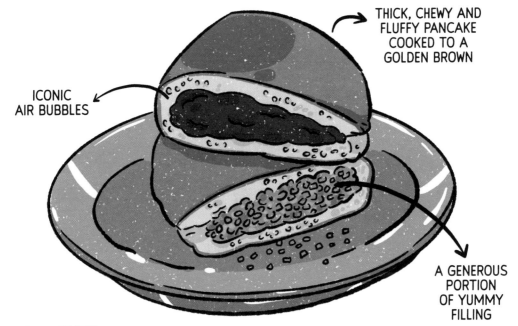

ICONIC
AIR BUBBLES

THICK, CHEWY AND
FLUFFY PANCAKE
COOKED TO A
GOLDEN BROWN

A GENEROUS
PORTION
OF YUMMY
FILLING

INGREDIENTS

Makes 1 pancake

73 g plain flour

37 g rice flour

½ tsp baking powder

⅛ tsp salt

1 egg

150 ml lukewarm water

1 Tbsp caster sugar

2 g instant dry yeast

Cooking oil, as needed

Filling of choice such as roasted chopped peanuts mixed with sugar, red bean paste, chocolate spread or cheese

MAKE THE PANCAKE

1. Combine the plain flour, rice flour, baking powder and salt in a mixing bowl. Set aside.

2. In another bowl, combine the egg, water, sugar and yeast. Mix until the sugar is dissolved.

3. Add this to the flour mixture and mix well. Cover the bowl with cling wrap and set aside in a warm place for 45 minutes.

4. In the meantime, prepare your choice of filling.

5. When ready to cook the pancake, heat a 25-cm non-stick pan over low heat. Brush well with oil.

6. Add enough batter to cover the base of the pan. Swirl the pan to spread the batter evenly.

7. When bubbles start to form and the pancake is lightly golden brown on the underside, spread some filling on the pancake and use a spatula to fold the pancake in half. Remove it from pan. Slice to serve and enjoy warm!

KITCHEN FUN FACTS

YEAST

Besides the colourful fillings, what makes a *min jiang kueh* different from regular pancakes? It is the *min jiang kueh's* chewier and thicker texture, thanks to the action of yeast.

Yeast is a living organism that thrives on sugar and moisture. When yeast is added to the batter, the enzymes in the yeast consume the sugar and create carbon dioxide in the process. When the batter is heated, the carbon dioxide rises and creates air pockets in the batter, making the pancake lighter and fluffier!

NASI LEMAK

This is one dish that can be said to excite all our senses! The steamed rice is rich with the fragrance of coconut milk and pandan leaves. The accompaniments of fried *ikan bilis* (anchovies) and peanuts are crisp and savoury. This is often paired with cucumber slices and a fried egg. At the side, the deep-red sambal chilli is sweetly spicy. To add to this palette of colours, smells, tastes and textures, *nasi lemak* is often served on a fresh banana leaf. A popular choice for breakfast (but also lunch and dinner!), *nasi lemak* can also be served with fried fish, *otak-otak* (grilled fish paste), chicken wings, sambal prawns, and the list goes on!

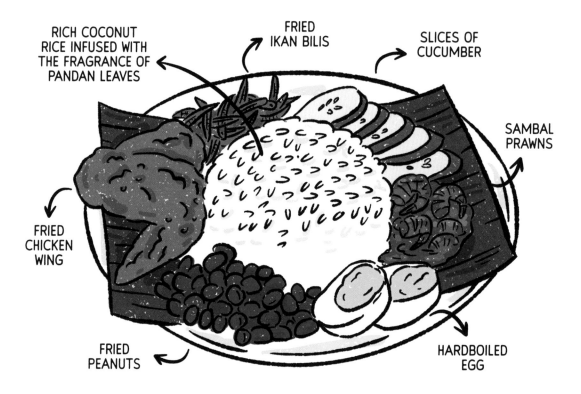

RICH COCONUT RICE INFUSED WITH THE FRAGRANCE OF PANDAN LEAVES

FRIED IKAN BILIS

SLICES OF CUCUMBER

SAMBAL PRAWNS

FRIED CHICKEN WING

FRIED PEANUTS

HARDBOILED EGG

INGREDIENTS

Makes 6 servings

2 cups Basmati rice

3-4 pandan leaves, cleaned and knotted

1 small knob ginger, skinned

625 ml coconut milk

SUGGESTED SIDES

- Sambal chilli
- Fried chicken wings
- Sambal prawns
- Crisp-fried *ikan bilis* (anchovies)
- Fried peanuts
- Hardboiled or fried egg
- Cucumber slices

COOK THE RICE

1. Rinse the rice and drain. Set aside.

2. To obtain coconut milk, add water to grated coconut and squeeze out the milk. For a quick fix, buy a carton of coconut milk from the supermarket.

3. Place the rice, pandan leaves, ginger and coconut milk in a rice cooker and cook. Serve the rice with a combination of the suggested sides.

KITCHEN FUN FACTS

THE RICE COOKER

With a rice cooker, rice can be prepared quickly and easily without much fuss. Prepare the rice and water according to the instructions provided by the manufacturer or the recipe and turn on the cooker. As the cooker heats up, the rice absorbs the water and turns out soft, fluffy rice or congee. Once all the rice is mostly cooked and there is no more water left, the temperature rises even more. The rice cooker senses the temperature automatically and stops cooking.

Besides cooking rice, the rice cooker can also be used to churn out oatmeal, risotto, soups, stews, steamed vegetables, pizza and even breads and cakes!

ONDEH-ONDEH

A good *ondeh-ondeh* has a thin layer of chewy dough that will burst and release all the sweet goodness of *gula Melaka* syrup inside your mouth. That's why it's recommended that you pop the whole *ondeh-ondeh* into your mouth and not bite or cut it. While green *ondeh-ondeh*, flavoured with pandan, is the most common, yellow, orange and purple ones can sometimes be found, due to the colour of the sweet potatoes used.

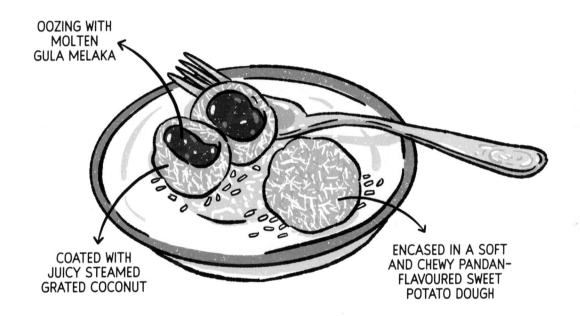

OOZING WITH MOLTEN GULA MELAKA

COATED WITH JUICY STEAMED GRATED COCONUT

ENCASED IN A SOFT AND CHEWY PANDAN-FLAVOURED SWEET POTATO DOUGH

INGREDIENTS

Makes 12 balls

140 g sweet potato

6 pandan leaves, cleaned and cut into short lengths

6 Tbsp water

6 Tbsp tapioca flour

¼ tsp salt

4 Tbsp *gula Melaka* (palm sugar), chopped

60 g skinned grated coconut

MAKE THE ONDEH-ONDEH

1. Boil the sweet potato for about 20 minutes until it is soft. Drain and peel. Discard the skin. Mash in a bowl and set aside.

2. Place the pandan leaves into a blender with 3 Tbsp water and process. Strain to obtain 3 Tbsp juice.

3. Add the tapioca flour, pandan juice and salt to the mashed sweet potato. Knead to get a soft and smooth dough. It should not be sticky.

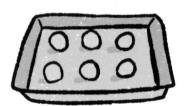

4. Divide the dough into 6 equal portions and roll each one into a ball.

5. Take a ball of dough and make a well in the centre. Spoon in some *gula Melaka* and seal. Repeat with the remaining ingredients.

6. Boil a pot of water and lower the balls in to cook. The balls will float when they are ready. Remove with a slotted spoon.

7. Mix the grated coconut with a pinch of salt. Steam for a few minutes. Roll the balls in the grated coconut. Enjoy!

KITCHEN FUN FACTS

KNEADING

Kneading is the action of squeezing and massaging dough to prepare it for the next step. To knead:

SHAPE THE DOUGH
INTO A BALL

PLACE THE HEEL OF YOUR HAND
ON THE BALL OF DOUGH BALL,
THEN PRESS DOWN AND
PUSH IT AWAY FROM YOU

FOLD THE DOUGH AND
CONTINUE TO PRESS DOWN
AND PUSH IT REPEATEDLY
UNTIL THE DOUGH REACHES THE
REQUIRED CONSISTENCY

Kneading ensures that the ingredients are well-mixed within the dough, and also helps incorporate air into it to give your final product a smooth and chewy texture.

PANDAN CHIFFON CAKE

Chiffon is a light fabric used to make clothing that is flowy and lightweight. So how did the term become synonymous with a cake? Could it be because chiffon cakes are light and fluffy, just like the fabric? Whatever the reason, the pandan chiffon cake is one of Singapore's favourite snacks today. It is available from cake shops, neighbourhood bakeries and supermarkets.

FRAGRANT WITH COCONUT MILK AND PANDAN JUICE

LIGHT AND FLUFFY GREEN COLOURED SPONGE

INGREDIENTS

Makes one 10-cm cake

EGG YOLK MIXTURE

6 pandan leaves, cleaned and cut into short lengths

2 tsp water

15 g caster sugar

2 egg yolks

2 Tbsp vegetable oil

70 ml coconut milk

1 tsp baking powder

⅛ tsp salt

⅓ tsp vanilla essence

40 g cake flour

MERINGUE

2 egg whites

45 g caster sugar

⅛ tsp cream of tartar

PREPARE THE EGG YOLK MIXTURE

1. Preheat the oven to 180°C. Prepare a 10-cm chiffon cake pan and set aside.

2. Place the pandan leaves into a blender with 2 tsp water and process. Strain to obtain 2 tsp juice. Set aside.

3. Using a wire whisk, beat the sugar and egg yolks for about 5 minutes until the mixture is pale and the sugar is dissolved.

4. Add the oil, coconut milk, baking powder, salt, pandan juice and vanilla essence.

5. Add the cake flour in 2 or 3 batches and mix until smooth. Do not over mix. Set aside.

PREPARE THE MERINGUE

1. Using an electric mixer, whisk the egg whites at low speed until foamy. Add the sugar and beat until soft peaks form.

2. Add the cream of tartar and beat at high speed for about 5 minutes until stiff peaks form.

BAKE THE CAKE

1. Fold the meringue into the egg yolk mixture in three batches. Pour the batter into a chiffon cake pan. Tap the pan lightly to release any air bubbles.

2. Place the cake in the oven and bake for 15–25 minutes or until a skewer inserted into the centre of the cake comes out clean. Invert the pan and let the cake cool completely before removing.

3. To release the cake from the pan, run a knife around the core and side of the pan. Invert onto a plate.

KITCHEN FUN FACTS

RAISING AGENTS

Just what is the secret behind getting a chiffon cake to be so tall, light and fluffy? The raising agents within the cake, that's what! Raising agents are ingredients that help baked products rise, by creating air bubbles during the baking process. Chemical raising agents include baking soda, baking powder and bread improvers. Naturally-derived raising agents are eggs and yeast.

In a chiffon cake, the egg whites help raise the cake when they are whisked to stiff peaks. The action of whisking introduces a lot of air into the egg whites which is then folded into the egg yolk mixture. When baked with other light ingredients like oil, the cake batter remains light and airy, the key elements of a delicious chiffon cake!

QING TANG (CHENG TNG)

This local dessert is yummy and easy to make, and can be found at many dessert stalls all around Singapore. What's more, it can be enjoyed either hot or cold to suit any preference! Made with a combination of healthy ingredients that are rich in vitamins and minerals, have anti-inflammatory properties, or can relieve dry or sore throats, this is a perfect example of having your cake and eating it too!

CLEAR SWEET SYRUP

CHOCK-FULL OF YUMMY, HEALTHY INGREDIENTS

INGREDIENTS
Makes 4 servings

4 malva nuts (*pang da hai*)

12 red dates

90 g pearl barley

50 g white fungus

12 ginkgo nuts

60 g dried longan

180 g rock sugar

2.5 litres water

45 g sago pearls

MAKE THE DESSERT

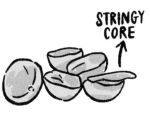

1. Soak the malva nuts in warm water until they swell. Remove the husks. Set the jelly aside.

2. Rinse the red dates, barley and white fungus.

3. Break the ginkgo nuts in half. Remove and discard the stringy core.

STRINGY CORE

4. Put the malva jelly, red dates, barley, white fungus, ginkgo nuts, dried longan and rock sugar into a big pot. Add the water and bring it to the boil.

5. When the water is boiling, add the sago. Lower the heat to a simmer, stirring occasionally for 15-30 minutes.

6. Remove from heat and serve hot or chilled.

KITCHEN FUN FACTS

BOILING

Boiling is a cooking method where water is heated to its boiling point (100°C). Foods submerged in the boiling water is cooked from the heat, and this includes meats and vegetables, eggs and grains.

Boiling can be done over low heat, which cooks the food, usually meats, slowly, resulting in a very tender final dish. Boiling can also be done over high heat to break down starches such as rice or pasta, or to cook tough vegetables such as potatoes and carrots until they are tender.

ROTI JALA

Have you had this pretty little snack before? These pancakes are light, savoury and a little chewy. *Jala* means "net" in Malay, and we can understand why these pancakes were so-named when we look at their lacy, net-like pattern. *Roti jala* is sometimes available from Malay food stalls, but as is it not very common, try making your own using this recipe.

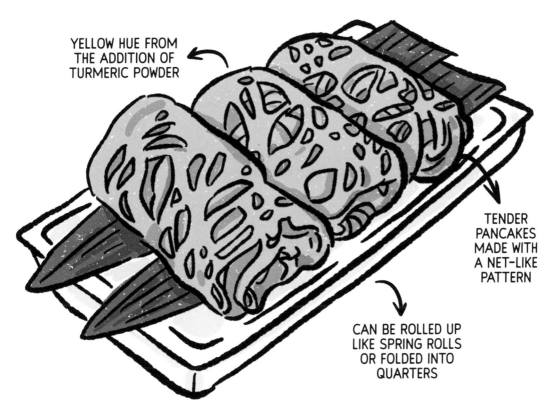

YELLOW HUE FROM THE ADDITION OF TURMERIC POWDER

TENDER PANCAKES MADE WITH A NET-LIKE PATTERN

CAN BE ROLLED UP LIKE SPRING ROLLS OR FOLDED INTO QUARTERS

INGREDIENTS

Makes 10

100 g plain flour

⅛ tsp turmeric powder

⅛ tsp salt

1 egg

1 tsp cooking oil + more for cooking

70 ml water

130 ml coconut milk

PREPARE THE BATTER

1. Sift the flour, turmeric powder and salt into a bowl.

2. Mix the egg, oil, water and coconut milk in another bowl. Add to the flour mixture and mix well.

3. Strain the batter through a sieve to remove any lumps. Pour the batter into a squeeze bottle.

COOK THE PANCAKES

1. Heat a little oil in a frying pan over medium heat. Squeeze the batter into the pan, creating a lacy pattern.

2. When the colour changes (this will take about 2 minutes), remove the pancake.

ROLL THE PANCAKES

1. Roll the pancake up while warm. Fold the two sides towards the centre, then roll up from the end nearest you. Serve with your favourite curry.

KITCHEN FUN FACTS

SIEVES AND STRAINERS

Sieves and strainers are essential tools in the kitchen.

Sieves are used to sift fine dry ingredients such as flours and powders to aerate them and break up any lumps. Strainers are used to separate solids from liquid ingredients.

In this recipe for *roti jala*, the batter is squeezed through a nozzle, so it needs to be very smooth to avoid choking the nozzle. Straining the batter will help us achieve that.

SATAY

Flavourful, tender and juicy, satay is seasoned meat threaded onto bamboo skewers and grilled over charcoal. It can be made using chicken, beef or pork, and is served with its signature savoury peanut sauce with cucumber, onion and compressed rice cakes on the side.

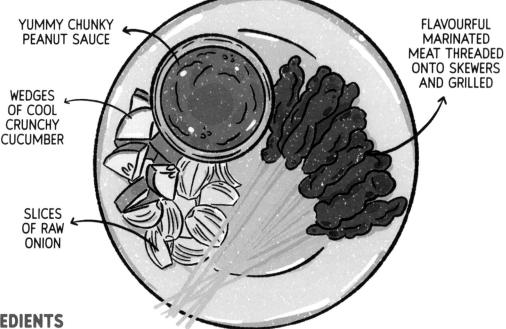

YUMMY CHUNKY PEANUT SAUCE

WEDGES OF COOL CRUNCHY CUCUMBER

SLICES OF RAW ONION

FLAVOURFUL MARINATED MEAT THREADED ONTO SKEWERS AND GRILLED

INGREDIENTS

Makes 8 sticks of satay

SATAY

200 g boneless chicken thigh meat

½ tsp turmeric powder

½ tsp ground cumin

2 Tbsp brown sugar

½ Tbsp cooking oil

1 Tbsp light soy sauce

¼ stalk lemongrass, bulbous end

1 small onion, peeled

1 clove garlic, peeled

PEANUT SAUCE

20 g dried chillies, soaked to soften

6 cloves garlic, peeled

100 g onion, peeled

30 g lemongrass

20 g galangal, peeled

100 ml cooking oil

200 g crushed peanuts

300 ml water

60 g *gula Melaka* (palm sugar)

2 tsp salt

PREPARE THE SATAY

  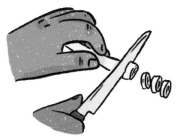

1. Soak 4–5 bamboo skewers in water to prevent them burning when grilled. Cut the chicken into small cubes about 2 x 2-cm.

2. Place the chicken cubes in a bowl. Add the turmeric powder, ground cumin, brown sugar, oil and light soy sauce. Mix well.

3. Slice the lemongrass, onion and garlic, then mince finely. Add to the chicken and mix well. Cover and set aside for 30 minutes.

4. Divide the chicken into 4–5 portions and thread onto the skewers. Preheat the oven to 200°C. Grill the satay for about 20 minutes or until meat is well done. Serve with satay sauce.

PREPARE THE SAUCE

1. Place the soaked dried chillies, garlic, onion, lemongrass, galangal and oil in a blender and process until smooth.

2. Transfer to a pan and cook, stirring over low heat. Add the remaining ingredients and cook to your desired consistency.

KITCHEN FUN FACTS

GRILLING

Although traditional satay is cooked over charcoal heat, grilling in the oven is a perfectly viable option for making this yummy dish at home. Just use the grill and fan mode and adjust the temperature to a minimum of 200°C. This will mimic the grilling action done over flames.

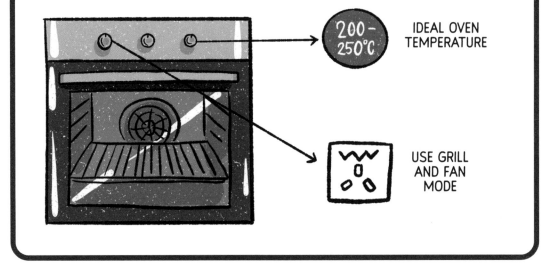

200 - 250°C — IDEAL OVEN TEMPERATURE

USE GRILL AND FAN MODE

IN THE 1970S IN SINGAPORE, SATAY WAS SOLD BY TRAVELLING HAWKERS WHO WENT FROM STREET TO STREET CARRYING THEIR COOKING EQUIPMENT AND INGREDIENTS IN BASKETS HUNG ACROSS THEIR SHOULDERS ON WOODEN POLES

TODAY, SATAY STALLS ARE LOCATED IN HAWKER CENTRES

TANG YUAN

These glutinous rice balls symbolise togetherness and unity in Chinese culture, and are traditionally served in sweet syrup to celebrate the Dongzhi (winter solstice) Festival. Today, these rice balls are available throughout the year and can be enjoyed as a snack at any time of the day. Traditional *tang yuan* are plain, but modern creations feature a variety of fillings from peanut paste to chocolate. You can even have them in all colours of the rainbow!

BALLS CAN BE LARGE OR SMALL, PLAIN OR COLOURFUL

SOFT AND CHEWY BALLS FLOATING IN SYRUP

LIGHTLY SWEETENED PANDAN FLAVOURED SYRUP

INGREDIENTS

Makes 10–20 balls, depending on size

50 g glutinous rice flour

7–8 tsp food colouring (see chart)

SYRUP

3 pandan leaves, cleaned and knotted

1 large piece rock sugar

500 ml water

NATURAL FOOD COLOURING OPTIONS

Purple	8 tsp blueberry purée from blending 1 Tbsp blueberries
Blue	7 tsp liquid from soaking 3–4 dried blue pea flowers in 7 tsp hot water
Green	5 tsp pandan juice from blending 10 pandan leaves with 2 tsp water
Yellow	8 tsp beaten egg yolk
Orange	8 tsp carrot juice from blending 1 medium carrot
Red/Pink	8 tsp red dragonfruit juice from blending 1 small red dragonfruit

PREPARE THE DOUGH

1. Prepare the food colouring according to the chart.

2. Measure out 50 g glutinous rice flour for each colour. Add the food colouring a little at a time and knead until the dough comes together.

3. Take a small lump of dough and roll it into a ball. Repeat for the remaining dough.

4. At this point, you can also add filling. Make a well in the centre of the ball and spoon some peanut or red bean paste into the well. Seal.

PREPARE THE SYRUP

1. Boil water over high heat. Add the pandan leaves and rock sugar.

2. When the sugar is dissolved, add the rice balls. They will float when done.

KITCHEN FUN FACTS

NATURAL FOOD COLOURING

Besides commercial food colouring, natural food ingredients provide a wealth of colouring options in every shade. Here are some suggestions on ingredients to use and the resulting colours. Now you can cook the rainbow!

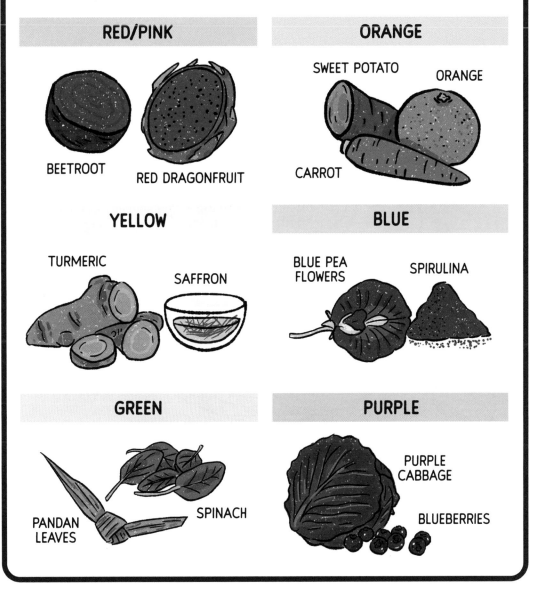

RED/PINK

BEETROOT RED DRAGONFRUIT

ORANGE

SWEET POTATO ORANGE CARROT

YELLOW

TURMERIC SAFFRON

BLUE

BLUE PEA FLOWERS SPIRULINA

GREEN

PANDAN LEAVES SPINACH

PURPLE

PURPLE CABBAGE BLUEBERRIES

KEROPOK UDANG

This savoury, crispy and flavourful snack must surely be Asia's answer to chips and crisps! If the word *keropok* reminds you of the sound made when one bites into a cracker, you might just be right! It's possible that's how it got its name *kerupuk* (or *krupuk*) in Indonesia where this snack originates. There are many types of *keropok,* but the most popular variety in Singapore is *keropok udang* or prawn crackers. Although it's readily available in supermarkets, nothing beats the experience of making your own!

IRRESISTIBLY CRISP AND FRAGRANT

TYPICALLY LIGHT PINK IN COLOUR DUE TO THE PRAWN PASTE

INGREDIENTS

Makes about 50 prawn crackers

200 g prawn meat, finely minced

250 g tapioca flour

1 tsp salt

1 Tbsp sugar

Cooking oil for deep-frying

PREPARE THE KEROPOK

1. Mix the prawn meat, tapioca flour and salt in a bowl.

2. Shape the mixture into 2 rolls. Steam for 45 minutes–1 hour until the rolls look a little translucent.

3. Let the rolls cool completely before refrigerating for an hour. Transfer to the freezer for 30 minutes.

4. When the rolls are sufficiently hardened, slice them as thinly as possible. The next step is to dehydrate the slices, either in the oven or by sunning.

5a. IN AN OVEN: Spread the slices out on a baking tray. Bake at 100°C for at least an hour, turning the slices over every 20 minutes or until crisp.

5b. IN THE SUN: Lay the slices out on a large tray and sun-dry for several days or until the slices are hardened and will snap upon bending.

6. Heat oil for deep-frying. Lower 2–3 slices into the hot oil each time. They will expand rather quickly. Drain well and store in an airtight container.

KITCHEN FUN FACTS

DEHYDRATING

The secret to making crispy *keropok* is to dehydrate or dry the slices as much as possible. The less moisture, the crispier the cracker! In some old neighbourhoods, you might still see large trays of *keropok* being laid out to dry in the sun. See if you can spot any the next time you're out! Yums!

VADAI

Pronounced "var-day", this classic South Indian snack is like a savoury doughnut. There are many types of *vadai* and they could be made from soaked and ground pulses, a variety of flours or even vegetables like potatoes. Some are also topped with prawns or *ikan bilis* (anchovies)! These tasty fritters can be eaten on their own or dipped into dals, chutneys or curries.

THIN, LIGHTLY CRISP, GOLDEN BROWN CRUST

SOFT AND FLUFFY INSIDE

FRAGRANT WITH SPICES

INGREDIENTS

Makes 15–20 vadai

4–5 medium potatoes

1.5-cm knob ginger

4–5 cloves garlic

1 small lemon

Cooking oil, as needed

½ tsp mustard seeds

5–6 curry leaves, stems removed

1 tsp turmeric powder

Salt, as required

1 Tbsp finely chopped coriander leaves

180 g gram (*besan*) flour

1 tsp ground cumin

240 ml water or as needed

PREPARE THE INGREDIENTS

1. Bring a pot of water to the boil. Peel the potatoes and cook in the boiling water until tender. Drain and mash.

2. Skin the ginger using a spoon, then chop finely. Peel the garlic and mince. Set aside.

3. Squeeze the lemon to extract 1 Tbsp juice. Set aside.

MAKE THE DOUGH

1. Heat 1 Tbsp oil in a pan over medium heat. Add the mustard seeds and cook until the mustard seeds start to pop.

2. Add the curry leaves, chopped ginger and minced garlic. Sauté until fragrant.

3. Add ½ tsp turmeric powder, mashed potatoes, ⅛ tsp salt and coriander leaves. Mix well over low heat.

4. Add the lemon juice and mix well. Remove from the heat and set aside to cool.

5. In a bowl, mix the gram flour with the ground cumin, remaining ½ tsp turmeric powder and ⅛ tsp salt.

6. Add water to the gram mixture gradually while whisking until a smooth batter forms.

FRY THE VADAI

1. Roll the potato mixture into balls the size of ping-pong balls.

2. Coat the potato balls well with the batter.

3. Heat oil for deep-frying over medium heat. Gently lower in a few balls at a time and cook until golden brown and crisp.

4. Remove with a slotted spoon and drain well on paper towels. Enjoy warm.

KITCHEN FUN FACTS

HERBS & SPICES

Herbs and spices are nature's flavouring agents! They are used to create balance between ingredients and to enhance the flavour of foods. You'll find them used in both sweet and savoury dishes, from breads and cakes, to meats and sauces. This *vadai* recipe is an excellent example of how herbs and spices can be used to add taste and flavour to food.

Below are some of the more common herbs and spices used in the kitchen.

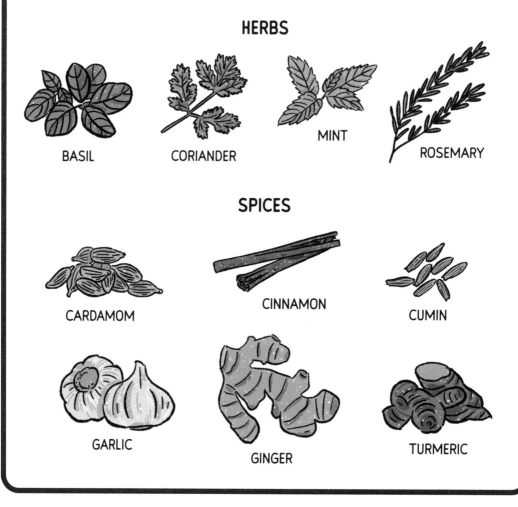

HERBS

BASIL   CORIANDER   MINT   ROSEMARY

SPICES

CARDAMOM   CINNAMON   CUMIN

GARLIC   GINGER   TURMERIC

WANTON MEE

What are the telling signs that a dish is truly Singaporean? When its name is a mixture of local dialects and languages! *Wanton* is the Chinese word for dumplings, while *mee* is the Hokkien word for noodles. There are numerous versions of dumpling noodles, especially in China, but this Singaporean dish is a different combination of magic!

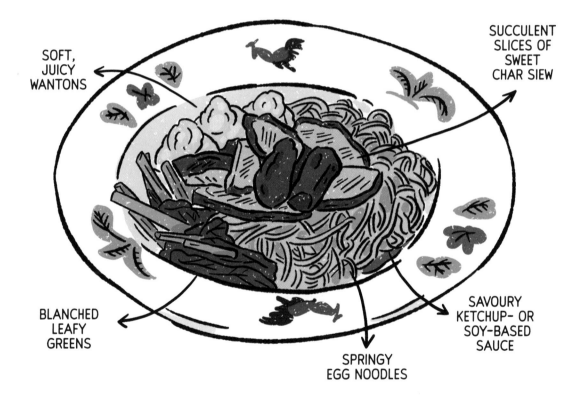

SOFT, JUICY WANTONS

SUCCULENT SLICES OF SWEET CHAR SIEW

BLANCHED LEAFY GREENS

SPRINGY EGG NOODLES

SAVOURY KETCHUP- OR SOY-BASED SAUCE

INGREDIENTS

Makes 1 serving

60 g egg noodles

1–2 stalks *kai lan*

SEASONING

1 tsp dark soy sauce

1 tsp light soy sauce

1 tsp oyster sauce

½ tsp sesame oil

½ tsp garlic oil

CHAR SIEW

100 g chicken thigh meat

1 tsp corn flour

⅛ tsp sugar

1 tsp light soy sauce

1 tsp dark soy sauce

1 tsp oyster sauce

1 tsp honey

WANTONS

40 g minced chicken

1 tsp sesame oil

1–2 tsp light soy sauce

½ tsp corn flour

1 tsp minced cabbage

6–8 *wanton* wrappers

PREPARE THE CHAR SIEW

1. Place the chicken meat in a bowl. Add corn flour, sugar, soy sauces and oyster sauce. Mix well and set aside for at least 15 minutes.

2. Preheat the oven to 190°C. Brush the chicken with honey. Place on a lined baking tray and grill for 10–20 minutes until the chicken is caramelised and cooked through. Slice before serving.

PREPARE THE WANTONS

1. Place the minced chicken in a bowl and season with the sesame oil, light soy sauce and corn flour. Mix in the cabbage and set aside for at least 15 minutes.

2. Spoon a teaspoonful of the chicken mixture onto a *wanton* wrapper. Fold the skin in half to get a triangle and seal with a little water. Repeat to make more.

3. Boil a pot of water and lower the dumplings in to cook. They will float when done. Remove with a slotted spoon and set aside.

PREPARE THE NOODLES AND GARNISHES

1. Prepare a deep serving plate and add the seasoning ingredients. Mix well and set aside. Boil a fresh pot of water and cook the noodles lightly. Remove with a strainer and place on the prepared serving plate. Toss to coat with the seasoning.

2. Return the water to the boil and blanch the *kai lan*. Remove with a strainer and plunge into a bowl of iced water to stop the cooking process. Drain and arrange on the serving plate with the noodles.

3. Arrange the *char siew* and *wantons* on the plate with the noodles and *kai lan*. Enjoy!

KITCHEN FUN FACTS

BLANCHING

Blanching is a quick-cooking technique where an ingredient is placed in a pot of boiling water, then removed after a short while. The ingredients can then be plunged into iced water to stop the cooking process. This ensures that the ingredients retain their colour, taste and nutrition!

XIAO LONG BAO

Originally from China, these soup dumplings are typically filled with pork, but our local spin on it has yielded chilli crab, seafood and even vegetarian options. The special feature of *xiao long bao* is the soup contained within each dumpling. So how is this done? This requires the additional step of freezing a gelatinised soup and enclosing it within the dumpling. Upon steaming, the gelatinised soup liquefies, creating that hot, soupy deliciousness! Did you know that the perfect *xiao long bao* must have thin skin and 18 folds, with a tiny crown at the top? It's definitely not an easy recipe to master, so here's a simplified version!

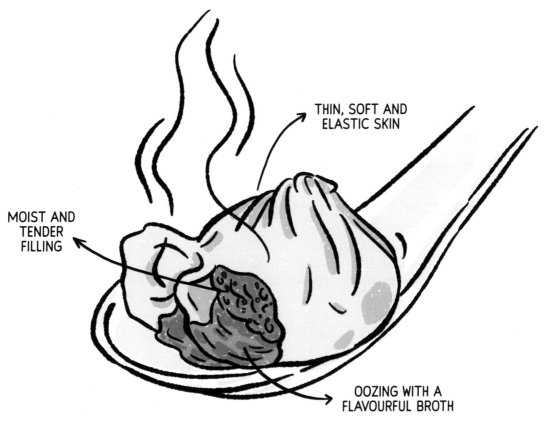

THIN, SOFT AND
ELASTIC SKIN

MOIST AND
TENDER
FILLING

OOZING WITH A
FLAVOURFUL BROTH

INGREDIENTS

Makes 16 dumplings

SOUP JELLY
1 tsp gelatin powder
1 Tbsp cold water
350 ml chicken stock

DUMPLING SKIN
150 g plain flour
80 ml hot water

FILLING
100 g minced chicken
½ tsp light soy sauce
¼ tsp sesame oil
½ tsp corn flour
½ medium carrot, peeled and finely chopped
2 tsp minced onion

GINGER AND VINEGAR
2.5-cm knob ginger, peeled and cut into fine matchsticks
2 Tbsp black vinegar

PREPARE THE SOUP JELLY

1. Do this a day ahead. Sprinkle the gelatine powder over the cold water in a bowl. Let it sit for 5–10 minutes until the water is fully absorbed and the mixture feels jiggly like jelly.

2. Bring the chicken stock to the boil, then let it cool until just warm. Add the gelatine and stir until fully dissolved. Let the stock cool completely before refrigerating overnight.

3. Measure out 128 g of the hardened soup jelly and cut it into small cubes. Set aside until needed.

PREPARE THE FILLING

1. Place the minced chicken in a bowl. Add the light soy sauce, sesame oil and corn flour. Mix well.

2. Add the chopped carrot and onion and mix well. Add the soup jelly cubes and mix well.

3. Divide the mixture into 16 portions.

PREPARE THE DUMPLING SKIN

1. Place the flour in a bowl. Gradually add the hot water and knead until a soft dough forms. Divide into 8 portions.

2. Roll a portion of dough into a ball. Use the ball of your palm to flatten it, then use a rolling pin to flatten the edges, turning the dough as you go to keep it round.

3. Place a portion of filling in the middle, then pleat the edges to seal. Try to form as many pleats as you can. Place in a lined steaming basket. Repeat with the remaining ingredients.

4. Steam the dumplings for 7 minutes. Serve immediately with finely sliced ginger and a dip of black vinegar.

KITCHEN FUN FACTS

MARINATING

Marinating is the process of soaking an ingredient, usually meat, in a sauce (or marinade) before cooking. When the meat is soaked in the marinade, it absorbs all the different flavours of the liquid. Generally, the longer the marination, the stronger the flavours will be. That is why some recipes call for the ingredient to be left in the marinade overnight. Depending on the ingredients used, marinating can also help tenderise or soften the meat.

Below are some of the most common types of ingredients used in marinades.

OILS AND SAUCES

HERBS AND SPICES

FRUITS

SEASONING

YOU CHAR KWAY

Have you ever wondered why this pastry is named *you char kway* or "fried devil"? The story is told how Yue Fei, a loyal Chinese general of the Song Dynasty, was on the verge of winning a battle against the enemy, when he was betrayed by his own prime minister, and subsequently executed. To express their anger at the injustice suffered by Yue Fei, the people made dough in two intertwined strips to represent the traitor and his wife (the *kway* or "devil"), and deep-fried (*you char*)them. Today, *you char kway* is a snack many enjoy for breakfast, paired with a bowl of hot soy bean milk. It is also commonly served with congee or *bak kut teh* (pork rib soup).

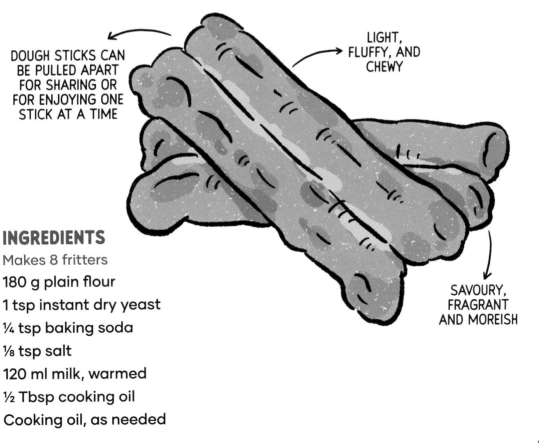

DOUGH STICKS CAN BE PULLED APART FOR SHARING OR FOR ENJOYING ONE STICK AT A TIME

LIGHT, FLUFFY, AND CHEWY

SAVOURY, FRAGRANT AND MOREISH

INGREDIENTS

Makes 8 fritters

180 g plain flour

1 tsp instant dry yeast

¼ tsp baking soda

⅛ tsp salt

120 ml milk, warmed

½ Tbsp cooking oil

Cooking oil, as needed

PREPARE THE DOUGH

1. Combine the flour, yeast, baking soda, salt, warmed milk and ½ Tbsp oil in a bowl.

2. Knead to get a soft dough, then cover and set aside in a warm place for 20 minutes.

3. Knead again until the dough is smooth. Dust a work surface and divide the dough into two. Flatten into rectangles.

4. Brush each portion of dough well with oil to prevent it from drying out.

5. Cover the dough with cling wrap and refrigerate for at least 2 hours.

6. When ready to cook, bring the dough back to room temperature. Cut each portion across into 8 strips.

SHAPE THE DOUGH

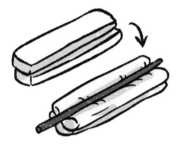

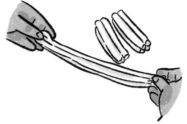

1. Place one strip of dough on top of another and press a chopstick down the middle lengthwise. This will keep the strips together.

2. Repeat with the remaining strips. Hold the two ends of a combined strip of dough and stretch until it is twice as long.

DEEP-FRY THE DOUGH

1. Heat oil for deep-frying over medium heat. Check that the oil is at the right temperature by dipping a dry wooden chopstick into the oil. Bubbles should start forming steadily around the chopstick.

2. Lower the stretched strip into the hot oil and deep-fry until the dough is fully expanded, and the fritter is crisp and golden brown.

3. Remove and set aside to drain. Repeat to stretch and deep-fry the remaining strips.

KITCHEN FUN FACTS

PROOFING

Proofing, sometimes also spelled proving, is a baking technique where dough is allowed time to rise to achieve a fluffy and airy final product.

When flour is mixed with yeast and water, and kneaded, the flour and water become elastic and stretchy due to the gluten in the flour. This gluten structure helps lock in the carbon dioxide produced by the yeast feeding on the sugars in the flour (or other ingredients), creating soft, airy dough.

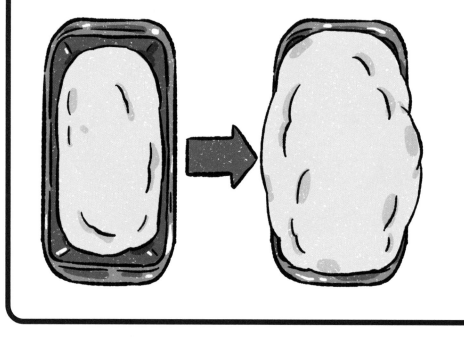

ZHU CHANG FEN

Also known by its Cantonese name, *chee cheong fun,* this yummy dish literally translates as "pig's intestine noodles". This is likely due to its rolled-up appearance, as it tastes nothing like pig's intestines. The thin, silky rice roll can be enjoyed plain or filled with a host of savoury fillings from prawns to chicken. It is usually served with a light savoury soy sauce and garnished with chopped spring onions.

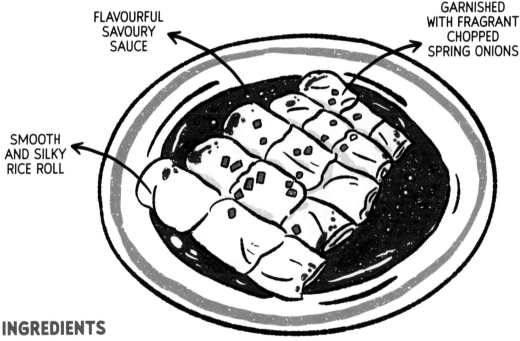

FLAVOURFUL SAVOURY SAUCE

GARNISHED WITH FRAGRANT CHOPPED SPRING ONIONS

SMOOTH AND SILKY RICE ROLL

INGREDIENTS
Makes about 10 rolls

RICE ROLL
120 g rice flour

10 g wheat starch flour

10 g tapioca starch

¼ tsp salt

1 Tbsp cooking oil

500 ml water

SAUCE
2 Tbsp light soy sauce

1 Tbsp sugar

2 Tbsp water

½ Tbsp sesame oil

PREPARE THE BATTER

1. Prepare a steamer and 2–3 steaming trays. Bring the water in the steamer to a rolling boil.

2. Combine the flours and salt in a bowl, then add the oil and water. Mix to get a runny batter.

3. Pour enough batter into a tray to cover the base of the tray.

STEAM THE BATTER

1. Place in the steamer, then cover and let it steam for 3–5 minutes, until the batter turns opaque and is set.

2. Using oven gloves, remove the tray from the steamer. Set aside to cool. Repeat to make more sheets using the other trays.

3. Let each sheet cool completely before using a spatula to ease it from the tray. Roll the sheet up and transfer to a serving plate.

4. Mix the ingredients for the sauce. Sprinkle spring onions over the rolls and drizzle with sauce. Serve warm.

KITCHEN FUN FACTS

DIM SUM

Zhu chang fen is a popular dim sum dish. But what exactly is dim sum? It is a concept and cuisine that originated in Guangzhou, China, centuries ago. Dim sum essentially consists of a wide range of bite-size dishes that can be enjoyed for breakfast, lunch or teatime with a pot of Chinese tea. Dim sum dishes can be steamed, baked or fried, and include buns, dumplings, tarts, cakes, rice, congees, soups, meats, puddings and desserts.

OUR
FAVOURITE
TREATS...

...FROM
ALL OVER
THE ISLAND

ABOUT THE AUTHOR AND ILLUSTRATOR

EMILY YEO

Although food was a great part of her life growing up, (#livetoeat) it was only out of necessity in her young adulthood that Emily set foot in the kitchen.

After deciding the corporate life was not for her, Emily took an early childhood education course and kickstarted a whole new teaching adventure that culminated in her establishing the culinary studio, The Little Things. Along the way, she has cooked and baked with thousands of children (including her own), learning and discovering numerous recipes. She has realised that the kitchen is indeed a treasure trove of lessons, with innumerable skills to hone and creative outlets to explore.

Emily's mission is to help everyone get a taste of the wonders and joys of food through her classes at The Little Things.

BENJAMIN WANG

Benjamin trained as a graphic designer but is an illustrator at heart. He runs Frus, a company that customises illustrations and designs handcrafted items, including plush toys, cards and tote bags. Benjamin believes food brings people together, and he hopes this book will spark many meaningful conversations and connections.